OBJECT ORIENTED PROGRAMMING IN C++

ARUN JOSEPH A KAVITHA S MURUGANANDHAM P

ISBN 979-888629063-9

Dedicated to the God Almighty my creator, my strong pillar, my source of inspiration, wisdom, knowledge and understanding. He has been the source of my strength throughout this program and on His wings only have I soared. I also dedicate this work to my friends and family members who has encouraged me all the way and whose encouragement has made sure that I give it all it takes to finish that which I have started.And i also dedicate my sincere thanks to the Authors of various sources who helped me to add their contents in this book.

Thank you.

Contents

Foreword

This book is intended for students in a variety of disciplines, including Computer Science, Information Technology, CT, and BCA programmes. The subject of C++ has been covered in accordance with the syllabi of several disciplines of Bharathiar universities. As a result, the book can be used in one semester of Computer Science streams, as well as in other degree and non-computer science courses. Object-Oriented Programming with C++ is a book for novices who have a basic understanding of C++ be an excellent text for those studying OOP. This book is for anyone who is looking for a unique way to express themselves to acquire and improve their C++ object-oriented programming skills.

The chapters are organised in a logical order. Each idea is described in an easy-to-understand manner, with multiple worked-out examples and programmes, in order to bridge the gap between theory and practise. This book's content was compiled from a variety of sources in order to help rural students improve their knowledge.

Preface

We live in a technologically advanced society where nearly everything is computerised. There have been numerous innovations throughout the previous two decades. It might be difficult for a novice to keep up with such changes. It might be frightening to get lost in a world of codes and bytes. This is where a textbook like this one comes in handy. This book takes the reader through the world of computers in a clear and organised manner, assuming no prior understanding of computers. Because computers cannot understand human speech, they require a communication medium in the form of a computer programming language to interact with them. C ++ is a programming language that is powerful, flexible, portable, and well-structured object oriented language.

Acknowledgements

I owe special thanks to the entire team of publishers. A note of acknowledgement is due to the reviewers for their valuable feedback. Their suggestions have helped in making the book more useful. This book is an honest attempt to leave a mark on the vast and infinite sands of knowledge. I would advise readers to take advantage of this work to the fullest extent possible. My heartfelt and sincere thanks to the authors of varius materials of publishers for allowing me to access the content.

Prologue

About the book

The chapters discuss the growth of the C++ programming language, object-oriented programming, and related concepts, as well as the drawbacks of traditional programming languages and C++ applications. This chapter delves into all of C++'s most important features. It covers inheritance, polymorphism, reusability, classes, and objects, among other C++ concepts. This chapter introduces object-oriented programming languages. The reader can follow the most fundamental input and output functions of the C++ language after becoming familiar with the concept of object-oriented paradigms in the previous chapter. Figures are used to explain streams, I/O functions, stream classes, buffers, typecasting, formatted and unformatted data, and functions. The majority of the notions are backed up by software. This ensures that the reader/programmer fully comprehends them. Furthermore, manipulators are discussed.

CHAPTER ONE

Syllabus

C++ PROGRAMMING

UNIT I: Introduction to C++ - key concepts of Object-Oriented Programming –Advantages – Object Oriented Languages – I/O in C++ - C++ Declarations. Control Structures : - Decision Making and Statements : If .. else ,jump, goto, break, continue, Switch case statements - Loops in C++ : for, while, do - functions in C++ - inline functions – Function Overloading.

UNIT II: Classes and Objects: Declaring Objects – Defining Member Functions – Static Member variables and functions – array of objects –friend functions – Overloading member functions – Bit fields and classes – Constructor and destructor with static members.

UNIT III: Operator Overloading: Overloading unary, binary operators – Overloading Friend functions – type conversion – Inheritance: Types of Inheritance – Single, Multilevel, Multiple, Hierarchal, Hybrid, Multi path inheritance – Virtual base Classes – Abstract Classes.

UNIT IV: Pointers – Declaration – Pointer to Class , Object – this pointer – Pointers to derived classes and Base classes – Arrays – Characteristics – array of classes – Memory models – new and delete operators – dynamic object – Binding, Polymorphism and Virtual Functions.

UNIT V: Files – File stream classes – file modes – Sequential Read / Write operations – Binary and ASCII Files – Random Access Operation – Templates – Exception Handling - String – Declaring and Initializing string objects – String Attributes – Miscellaneous functions .

TEXT BOOK:

1. Ashok N Kamthane, Object-Oriented Programming with Ansi And Turbo C++, Pearson Education, 2003.

REFERENCE BOOKS:

1. E. Balagurusamy, Object-Oriented Programming with C++, TMH, 1998.
2. Maria Litvin & Gray Litvin, C++ for you, Vikas publication, 2002.
3. John R Hubbard, Programming with C, 2nd Edition, TMH publication, 2002.

CHAPTER TWO

INTRODUCTION TO C++

1.1 Evolution of C++

- C++ is an object oriented language. It is consider to be extension of C.
- Bjarne Stroustrup at AT&T Bell laboratories, New Jersey (USA) develop in the 20th century.
- Stroustrup derived ideas from SIMULA67 and ALGOL 68 and developed a new language called "C with classes". In 1983 the name was changed to C++.
- C++ is a super set of c.

1.2 ANSI standard

- ANSI stands for american national standard institute was founded in 1918.
- The main goal is to reform recommend and publish standards for data processing in computer organization is USA.
- The ANSI provides the standard for C++ and also referred to ISO.

1.3 Programming Paradigms

Programming languages are classified into three types.

1. Monolithic programming
2. Procedural languages
3. Structured programming

1.3.1 Monolithic programming

- It contains global variable, jump statements. The statements are written is sequence.
- It does not support sub programming concept and hence useful for smaller programs.

Ex: BASIC AND ASSEMLY

1.3.2 Procedural programming

- The control of program is transferred using GOTO statement.
- Data is global and all the sub programs share the same data.
- These languages are used for developing medium size applications.

Ex: COBOL, FORTORAN.

1.3.3 Structured programming

- The programs are divided into multiple sub modules and procedures.
- Each procedure has to perform different tasks.
- Each module have local variables, user defined data types also used.

Ex: C and PASCAL

1.4 Disadvantage of Conventional Programming

The following drawbacks observed in monolithic procedural and structured programming language.

- Large sizes programs are divided into sub program know as function these function can call one another hence security in not provided.
- Data passes globally from one function to another.

2. KEY CONCEPT OF OBJECT ORIENTED PROGRAMMING (OOP)

2.1 Objects

- Objects are the primary runtime entities in an object oriented programming.
- Objects occupy space in memory.
- Every object has its own properties or functions.
- The action of the object depends upon the member function defined within its class.

Ex: Pen, Book, Computer, CPU etc,.

2.2 Classes

- A class is the accomplishment of abstract data type. It defines the nature and method that act on the data structure and abstract data type respectively.

- A Class is a grouping of objects. It has own property, common behavior and shared relationship.
- Classes define the characteristics and actions of different objects.

Ex:
Class : car
Properties : company, color, model, capacity
Actions : speed, average, break.

2.3. Method (functions)

- A function is a small program it performs a specific task when called from a class.
- An operation that is required for the objects are to be defined is a class.
- A class is associated with member variables and member functions (methods).

Ex:

```
Class BCA
{
private:
member variable1;
member variable2;
public:
member function1( ) or method1( )
{
}
};
```

2.4 Data abstraction

- Abstraction is to represent the important details or features without including the back ground details.
- Data abstraction is the procedure of identifying the properties and methods related to an object.

Ex: Computer àmethod board, ram, hard disk.

2.5 Encapsulation

- The packing of data and function into a single component is known as encapsulation.
- The data is not accessible by outside functions.
- The functions are defined within the class can access the data.

Ex: Mother board, ram, hard disdàcpu
Different dataàsingle component.

2.6 Inheritance

- Inheritance is a concept in which the properties of one class used by another class.
- It provides the thought of reusability.

Ex: Grandfather à Father à Son

2.7 Polymorphism

- Polymorphism is the same function to at differently in different classes.
- Polymorphism is derived from 2 Greek words: **poly** and **morphs**. The word "poly" means many and **morphs** means forms. So polymorphism means many forms.

Polymorphism

2.8 Dynamic Binding

- Binding means link between procedure call and code to be execute.
- Dynamic binding means link exist between procedure call and code to be execute at run time when that procedure is call.
- It is also known late binding.
- For example, complier comes to know at runtime that which function of sum will be call either with two arguments or with three arguments.

Ex:

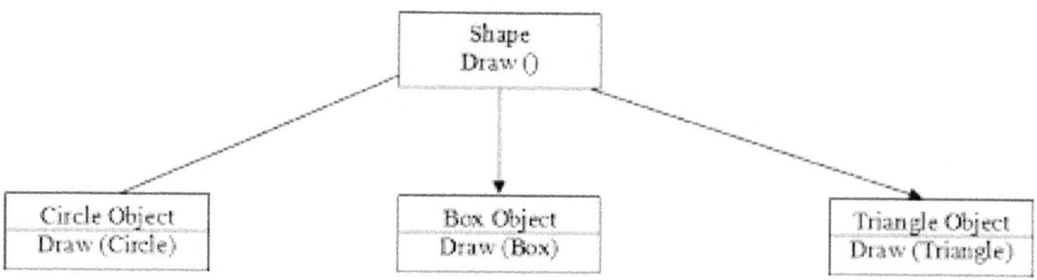

Data binding

2.9 Message Passing

- Object oriented programming includes objects which communicate with each other.

  The following steps used to be followed to communicate the objects:

1. Declaring classes that define the object and their action.
2. Declaring objects from the classes.
3. Implementing relation between objects.

Ex: Object.Memberfunction(arguments)

2.10 Reusability

- Reusability of the classes by extending them to the other classes using inheritance.

2.11 Delegation

- Delegation also reusability of the difference classes.
- In inheritance one class can be derived from other class and relationship between them is knows as kind of relationship.
- Relationship between two classes is known as has a relationship.

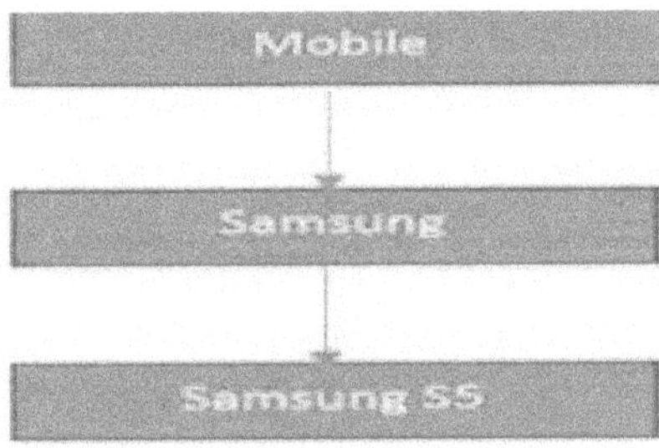

Delegation

2.12 Genericity

- The software component of a program has more than one version depending on the data types of arguments.
- The programmer can create a function that accepts any types of data is called template.

3. ADVANTAGES OF OOPS

- OOPs provide many advantages to the programmer.
- Object oriented programs can be comfortably upgraded.
- Using inheritance will avoid the rewriting of the program code.
- Data hiding method allows the programmer to design and develop the program is safe and security.
- The encapsulation feature allows the programmer to define classes with many functions.
- OOPs languages can created extended and reusable.
- Oops support to development of new software in short time

4. INPUT and OUTPUT IN C++

- C++ supports all input and output functions of C. C++ also has library functions
- A library is a set of .obj files, which is linked to the program.

- The library is also called as iostream library.

4.1 Streams in C++

- C++ supports a number if input/output operations to read and write operations
- The standard C++library contains the I/O stream functions.
- Streams are a class used to work with console and file operations.
- I/O stream.h is header files which declare the stream classes.
- The input stream uses cin object to read the data and the output stream uses cout object to display the data on the screen.
- The operator (<<insertion operator) is over loaded in ostream class.
- The operator (>>extraction operator) is over loaded in istream class.

Ex:

```
#include<iostream.h>
#include<conio.h>
Void main()
{
Int x;
Float y;
Char z;
Cout<<"enter the int , float and char value";
Cin>>n>>y>>z;
Cout<<"the values are";
Cout<<"x="<<x<<"y="<<y<<"z="<<z;
Getch();
}
```

Output:

enter the int , float and char value :10 51.5 c

x=10 y=15.5 z=c

4.5 Formatted and Unformatted Data

- Formatting means representation of data with different settings as per the requirement of the user. The various settings that can be done are number format, field width, decimal points etc.

- For an example if the user wants to display the data in hexa-decimal format then the manipulator can be used as follows,

```
cout<<hex<<15; ------> F
```

4.6 Unformatted console I/O operations

Input and Output Streams

- The input stream uses cin object to read data and the output streams uses cout object to display data on the screen.
- input stream: cin>>variable Ex: cin>>x
- ouput stream: cout<<variable. Ex: cout<<x

4.7 Type casting with cout statement

- Type casting refers to the conversion of data from one basic type to another by applying external use of data type keywords.

Ex:

```
void main()
{
int a=66, float f=2.4, char c='K';
clrscr();
cout<<" int in char format:"<<(char)a;
cout<<" float in int format:"<<(int)f;
cout<<" char in int format:"<<(int)c;
}
```

Output:

```
int in char format: B
float in int format: 2
char in int format: 75
```

4.8 Formatted Console input /output Operations:

C++ provides various formatted console I/O functions for formatting the output. They are of three types.

1. ios class function and flags
2. mainpulators
3. User defined output functions

Formatted functions with cout object

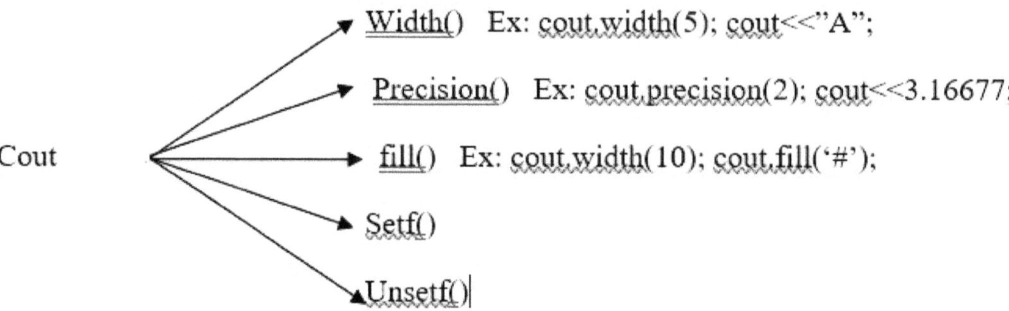

4.9 Bit Field with Flags

- The ios class function contains setf() member function. The flag used design the output. The unsetf() used to clear the flag.

Syntax:
Cout.Setf(v1.v2);
Cout.Unsetf(v1);

Flag(v1)	Bit field(v2)	Format
ios::left	ios::adjust field	Left justification
ios::right	ios::adjust field	Right justification
ios::dec	ios::base field	Decimal base
ios::oct	ios:: base field	Octal base
ios::hex	ios:: base field	Hexadecimal base

Table: Bit fields

Ex:

```
Void main() {
Clrscr();
Cout. Fill ("=");
Cout.setf (ios::right,ios::adjust field);
Cout.width(5);
Cout<<"C++";
Cout.set (ios::left,ios::adjustfied);
Cout.width(5);
Cout<<"C++";}
```

Output

C + + = =

= = C + +

4.10 Manipulators

- The output formats can be controlled using manipulator. The header file iomainp.h has a set of functions.

Syntax: Cout<<m1<<m2<<v1; where M1, m2->manipulator , V1->variable

Ex:

```
#include<iostream.h>
Void main()
{
int x=84;
Cout<<"x="<<x;
Cout<<"hexa-decimal="<<hex<<x;
Cout<<"octal number="<<oct<<x;
}
```

Output:

x=84 hexa-decimal=54 octal number=1

5. C++ DECLERATION

5.1 Parts of C++ Program

Include file
Class declaration or definition
Class function definition
Main() function

- Every C++ program starts with main() function without main() function the program will not be executed.
- C++ allows combining variable and function in structures and classes.

Include file

- C++ program depends upon some header files for function definition
- Each header file has an extension .h.
- **Ex:** #include<iostream.h> or #include"iostream.h"

Class declaration or definition

- Declaration of a class is done in this section.
- The class may be declared before the main function or after the main function.
- The class contains variables, functions prototypes or function definition.
- The class definition is always terminated by a semicolon.

Class function definitions

- The function definition can be done outside or inside of the class but the function should be declared inside of the class.

The main() function

- C++ program always start execution from main() function.

Ex:

```
#include<iostream.h> ----- header or include file
Class A ----- class declaration
{
Void sum() ----- function declaration & definition
{
int a=10, b=10; ----- class variables
int c=a+b;
Cout<<"c="<<c;
}
}; ----- end of the class
Void main() ----- main() function
{
A a; ----- creating an object for a class
a.sum();} ---- accessing member function of a class
```

Output

c=20

5.2 Types of Tokens

- C++ programs contain various components. The compiler identify them as tokens.
- The tokens are classified in the following types.

1. Key words
2. Variables
3. Operators
4. Constants
5. Special character

5.3 Key Words

- Key words are reserved words and have fixed meanings.
- The key words are cannot be used as variables.

Ex: Class private Delete public Friend Inline template
New try Operator throw Virtual protected this

5.4 Identifiers

- Identifiers are name of variables, functions and arrays.
- The variables are user-defined names, Sequence of letters and digits with a letter as a first character.
- The underscore(_) symbol can be used as an identifier.

Rules for Identifiers

- The identifier name stars with a character and should not start with a digit.
- Identifier should not use any special character except underscore symbol (_).
- The identifier name should not be a keyword.
- Identifier name may be a combination of upper and lower character.
- The identifier does not have any bound of length of character.

Ex:

1. Name valid identifier
2. $name invalid identifier
3. Student name invalid identifier
4. Class_ room valid identifier
5. Private invalid identifier
6. 5a invalid identifier
7. Roll number invalid identifier

5.4.1 Variable Declaration and Initialization

Variable

Variable declaration

- The variable must be declared before using it. In C++ declaration of variable anywhere in the program.
- The declaration of variable has name of the data type and variable name.

Syntax: Data type v1
Where Data type may be the primary data type and v1 is the name of the variable .
Ex: int a,b,c; Char d; Float f;
Initialization

- Assigning a value to the variable is called initialization.

Syntax: datatype vname= value or vname=value
Ex: int a=5; int a,b,c; a=b=c=5;

1. **Dynamic Initialization**

- The declaration and initialization of the variable in a single statement at any place in the program is called dynamic initialization.

Ex:

```
Void main()
{
int r;
cout<<"enter the radius";
cin>>r;
Float area=3.14*r*r;
Cout<<"\n area ="<<area;
}
```

5.6 Data Types in C++

- Data is a collection of characters, digits, symbols etc.,
- It is used to represent information.
- C++ data types are classified in the following categories.

1. Basic data type
2. Derived data type

3. User-defined type
4. Void data type

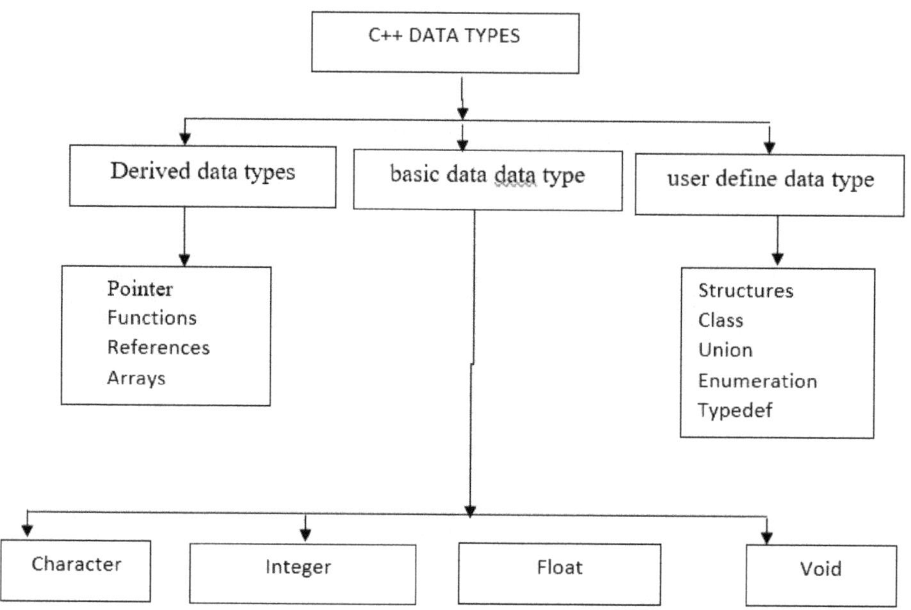

5.7 Basic Data Type

- Basic data types are used to declare the variable.

Char
1 byteà -128 to +127 (range)
Char à 1 byte
Unsigned char à 1 byte
Signed char à 1 byte
Integer
Integer à 2 bytes short à 2 bytes longà4 bytes

Signed int à 2 bytes unsigned short à2 bytes unsigned long à4 bytes
Unsigned int à 2 bytes signed short à2 bytes signed long à4 bytes

Float

Float à 4 bytes
Double à 8 bytes
Long double à 10 bytes

Boolean

Bool à 1 bytes (true or false)

5.8 Derived Data Types

The derived types are of following types.

1. Pointer
2. Function
3. Arrays
4. References

1. **Pointers**

- A pointer is a memory variable that stores a memory address of another variable.
- It is declared as a normal variable but it is denoted by ' * ' operator.

Ex:

```
int a, *x;
a=10;
x=&a;
```

2. **Function:**

- A function is a self-contained block or a sub-program of one or more statements that perform a task when called.

Ex:

```
Void main()
{
Show();
}
```

```
Void show();
{
Cout<<"C++ programming";
}
```

3. **Array**

- Array is a collection of data item of same data types in which each element is located in separate memory location.

Ex:

```
Void main()
{
int a[30];
A[3]={10, 20, 30};
Cout<<"a[2]<<a[0]<<a[1];
}
```

Output: 30 10 20

4. **References**

- C++ reference types, declared with & operator are nearly identical but not exactly same to pointer types.
- They declare aliases for object variables and allow the programmer to use variable by reference.

5.9 User Defined Data Types

User defined data types are of the following types.

1. Structures and classes
2. Union
3. Enumerated data types

1. **Structures and classes**

i.Structures

- Structure is a collection of different data type members into a single record with separate memory location.

Syntax:

```
Struct struct_name
{
(data-type) variable;
}Structure variable decleration;
```

Ex:

```
Void main()
{
Struct books
{
int bno =100;
float rate;
char name[20];
}b1;
Cout<<b1.b no;
}
```

Output: 100

ii.Classes

- Class is a collection of object, member variables and member functions.

Syntax:

```
Class class_name
{
member variable;
member function;
}
```

Ex:

```
Class BCA
{
int a=45;
float b=a/10;
Void show()
{
cout<<a<<b;
```

```
}};
Void main()
{
BCA s;
s.show();
}
```

Output: 45 4.5

2. **Union**

- Union is the collection of different data type members in a single record with shared memory location.

  Syntax

```
Union union_name
{
(data type) variable – name;
}union variable;
```

  Ex:

```
Void main()
{
Union book
{
int bno=100;
float rate;
}b1;
Cout<<b1.b no;
}
```

Output: 100

3. **Enumarated data type**

- The user can declare the new data type and define the variables in that data type using the key word enum.

  Syntax:

```
Enum logical (false, true);
```

The answer is o or where in the false or true.

Ex:

```
Void main()
{
clrscr();
enum logical (false, true);
cout<<"true="<<true<<"false="<<false";
}
```

Output: true=1 false=0

5.10 Void Data Type:

- Void is a data type it is used to define the function return type.
- If the return type is void the function does not return any value.

Eg:

void show (int a)

The function show does not return any value to the main function.

int add (void)

The function add does not receive any value from main () function.

5.11 Type Modifiers

- A type modifier changes the meaning of the basic data type to produce new data type.
- The short long signed and unsigned are the type modifiers.

Ex:

```
Void main()
{
Short a=1;
Long m=66677;
Signed j=10;
Cout<<"l"<<"m"<<"j"<<;
}
```

Output: l=1 m=66677 j= --10

5.12 Wrapping Around

- A variable contain a value which goes over the range provided by the computer.
- The computer does not display any error and wrapping around takes places.

Ex:

```
Void main()
{
Clrscr();
Unsigned int x=65535;
Cout<<"x="<<x;
}
```

Output: x=0

5.13 Type Casting

- Type casting is the process to convert one data type to another data type.
- C++ support implicit and explicit type conversions.

i. Explicit type casting (or) type conversion

- The explicit type conversion is done using type cast operator.

Syntax:

Data – type name (expression)

Ex:

```
x=5/float (2); x=5/2.0; x=2.5; int (x)=2;
Void main()
{
Float x;
x=5/float (2)
Cout<<x=<<x;
Cout<<x=<<int (x);
}
```

Output: x=2.5 x=2

ii.implicit type conversion

- The type conversion carried out when the expression contains different types of data items. Compiler carries conversion operation.
- The conversion of lower data type to higher data type is known as promotion.
- The conversion of higher data type to lower data type is known as demotion.

Ex:

```
int a=50;
float (a)=50.0 ----------promotion
float a=32.5
int (a)=32--------------------------demotion
Void main()
{
int j=2.54;
int k=a;
char c=87;
cout<<"j="<<j;
cout<<"k"<<k;
cout<<"c="<<c;
}
```

Output:

j=2
k=65àANSI code of a
c=w (87th ANSI character)

5.14 Constant

- The constants value which do not change during the execution of a program.
- C++ has two types of constant

i. literal constant
ii.symbolic constant

i. literal constant

- A literal constant is directly assigned to a variable.

Ex: int j=20;

Where j is the variable of type int and 20 is a literal constant. The value 20 cannot be change.

ii. symbolic constant

- The symbolic constant is defined as the variable after initialization of constant the assigned value cannot be change.
- The symbolic constant defined is three ways.

define **ex:** #define N=10

const **ex:** const int X=10

The enum key words **ex:** enum {a,b,c}

```
#define N 5
Void main()
{
Const int k=2;
Cout<<"N="<<N;
Cout<<"K="<<K++;
}
```

Output:

N=5

Error message (const value cant be changed)

5.15 Operators in C++

Type of Operators	Symbolic Representations
Arithmetic Operator	+ - * / %
Relational Operator	> >= < <= == !=
Logical Operator	&& || !
Increment and decrement Operator	++ --
Assignment Operator	=
Bitwise Operator	& \ ^ >> << ~
Special Operator	,
Conditional Operator	?:

5.16 Referencing (&) and Dereferencing Operators (#)

referencing operator (&)

- Referencing operator is used to define the referencing variables.
- A reference variable prepares an alternative (alias) name of previously defined variable.

Syntax: Data type & reference variable name = variable name

Ex: int a=10; int & b=a;

dereferencing operator (*)

- The dereferencing operator (*) displays the value of the referencing variable and this variable also called pointer variable.

Ex:

```
Void main()
{
```

```
int a=10;
cout<<"address of a="<<(&a);
cout<<"value of a="<<(*(&a));
}
```

Output:

address of a=98977

value of a=10

5.17 Scope Access Operator

- The declaration of a variable are member function inside the class can accessed only in inside of the class but these members also can be accessed by the outside of the class with the help of scope access operator.
- The scope access operator allows the programmer to access a global variable even it is hidden by local re-declaration.

Ex:

```
int a=20;
Void main()
{
int a=10;
Cout<<"::a="<<::al
Cout<<"a="<<a;
}
```

Output: ::a=20 a=10

5.18 Memory Management Operator:

- In C++ provides operator that allocate and release the memory.
- The memory management operators are **new** and **delete.**

new : Create an object , allocate the memory location

delete : Re-allocate the memory location, Destroy the object

The Advantages of New Operator

- The new operator itself calculate the size of the object without the use of size of () operator
- It returns the pointer type.
- The new operator allocates memory and initialize the object at once.

Syntax: Pointer memory variable = new data type (size);

- Here pointer memory variable is a pointer to the data type. New operator allocates memory on specified data type and return back to the starting address.

Ex:

```
int * p = new int [3]
p = new int;
*p = new int [3];
```

Delete Operator

Syntax: Delete pointer memory variable.

Ex: Delete p

5.19 Comma Operator

- C++ allows to terminate a statement using comma operator after satisfying the following rules.

1. The variable declaration statements should be terminated by semicolon.
2. The statement followed by declaration statements like clrscr(), cin and cout can be terminated by comma operator.
3. The last statement of the program must end with semicolon.

```
void main ()
{
int a;
clrscr();
cout<<"enter value a",
Cin>>a,
int b=a*a;
cout<<"b="<<b;
getch();
}
```

5.20 Comma in place of Curly Brace

The curly braces{ } are used to define the starting and ending of the function. It is also possible to use comma in condition and loop statement in place of { }.

```
Void main ()
```

```
{
int a;
clrscr ();
cout<<"enter the value a";
cin>>a;
if (a = = 10)
cout<<"a="<<a*2,
else
cout<<"a="<<a*3,
getch();
}
```

6. **CONTROLSTRUCTURES**

- A Program is a sequence of coding which execute line by line but the programmer can alter the flow of executing using control structures.

Decision making statements

- The C++ control structure is a set of code that makes decision is called decision making statements. The decision making statements are,

- if statement
- switch statement

1. Simple if statement

- The simple if statement is contain an expression.
- The expression evaluated. If the expression is true it returns 1 otherwise 0.
- When the expression is true the statement in if block is executed and when the expression is false then the if block is skipped and statement after if is executed.

Syntax:

```
if (test expression)
{
statement-1 (if block);
```

}

Flow chart:

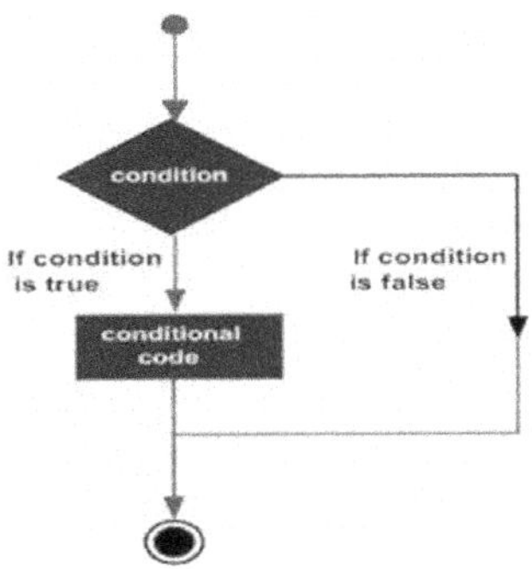

Example:

void main()

int a;

cout<<:Enter a :";

cin>>a;

if(a>5)

{

cout<<"\n a isgreater than 5"; **output:**

}

cout<<"\n end of the program; Enter a: 10

getch(); a is greater than 5

} end of the program

2. if .. else statement

- if statement is contain an expression. When the expression is true the statement in if block is executed and when the expression is false the statement in else block is executed.

syntax

if (test expression)

{

statement-1 (if block);

```
}
else
{
statement-2 (else block);
}
```

Flow chart:

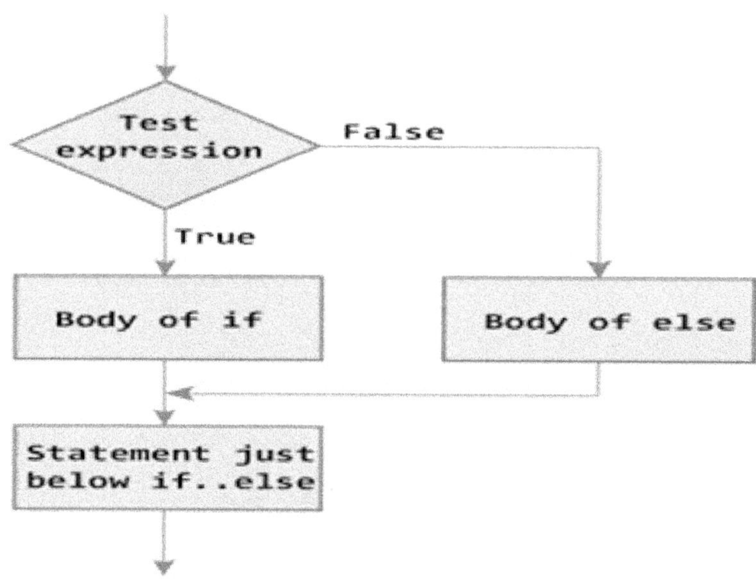

Figure: Flowchart of if...else Statement

Example:

```
void main()
int a,b;
cout<<"Enter a anb b values :";
cin>>a>>b;
if(a>b)
{
cout<<"\n a is greater than b";
```

output:

} Enter a anb b values : 6 7
else a is less than b
{ end of the program
cout<<"\n a is less than b";
}
cout<<" end of the program";
getch();
}

3. The nested if.. else statement

- The nested if else number of logical conditions is checked for executing various statements. If any logical condition is true then the if block is executed otherwise it skips and executes else block.

syntax:

```
if(test exp1)
{
if(text exp2)
{
statement-1;
}
else
{
statement-2;
}
else
{
statement3;
}
```

Flow chart:

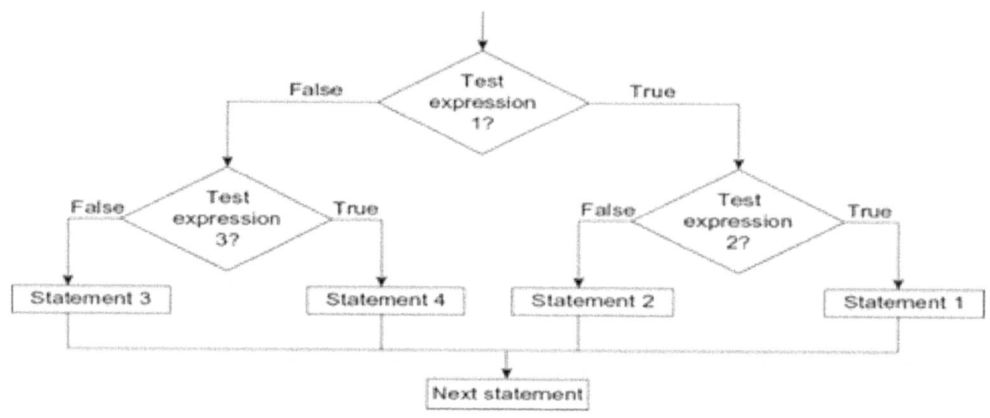

Enter Caption

example:

```
void main()
{
int a,b,c;
cout<"\n Enter a,b,c:";
cin>>a>>b>>c;
if(a>b)
{
if(a>c)
{
cout<<"\n A is greater than b and c";
```

output:

```
} Enter a,b,c : 25 20 30
else a is less than c
{
cout<<"\n A is greater than c";
}
else
{
cout<<"\n a is less than b";
```

}

4. Else if ladder

- The else if ladder is a multi-way decision making statement which check the multiple conditions and execute only the true condition. If none of the conditions are true it execute else block.

syntax:

```
if( test exp1)
{
statement-1
}
else if(test exp-2)
{
statement-2
}
else if(test exp3)
{
statement-3
}
else
{
statement-x
}
```

Flow chart

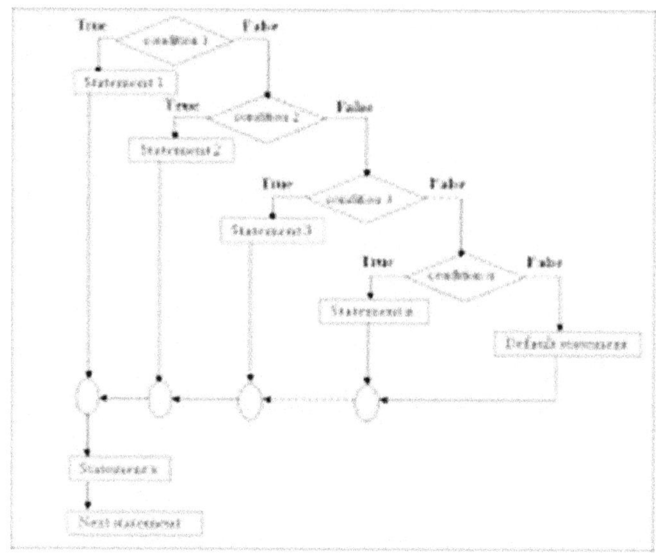

Example:

```
void main()
{
int mark;
cout<<"Enter mark:";
cin>>mark;
if(mark>80)
{
cout<<"grade A+";
}
else if(mark>70)
{
cout<<"grade A";
}
else if(mark>60) output:
{ Enter mark: 78
cout<<"grade b"; grade A
```

}
else Enter mark: 49
{ no grade
cout<<"no grde";
}

5. Switch case statement

- The switch statement is a multi-way branch statement. In switch statement check the numbers of case options if the value is matched with case constant then the corresponding case is executed until the break statement is found.

syntax

```
switch variable(or) expression
{
case constant A:
statement-1;
break;
case constant B:
statement-2;
break;
default:
statement-x;
}
```

Flow chart

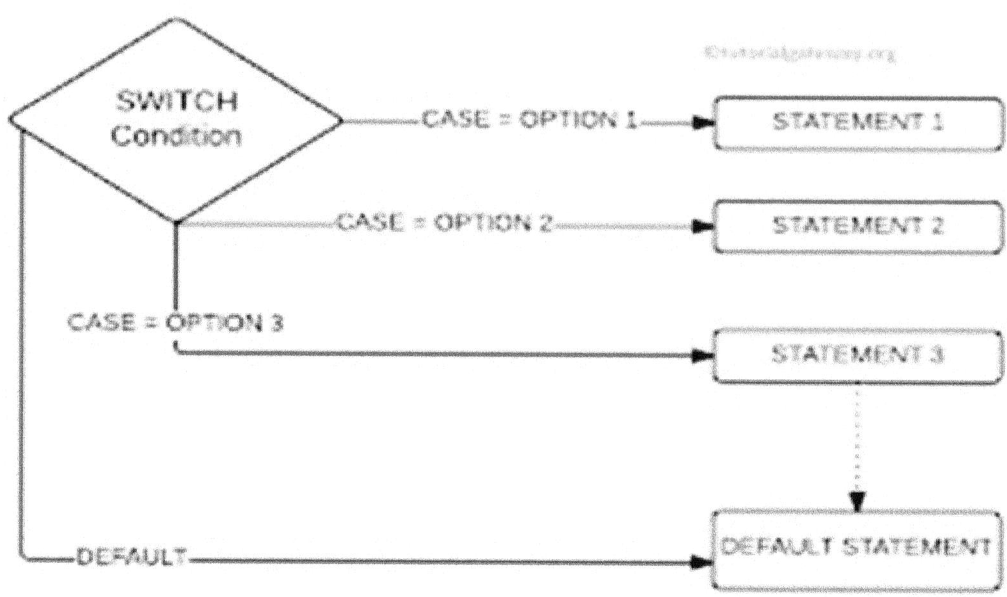

Example:

```
void main()
{
char a;
clrscr();
cout<<"Enter any alphabet:";
cin>>a;
switch(a)
{
case 'A'||'a'
cout<<"A";
break;
case 'E'||'e'
cout<<"E";
break;
```

```
case ‘I’||’i’
cout<<”I”;
break;
case ‘O’||’o’
cout<<”O”;
break;
case ‘U’||’u’
cout<<”U”;
break;
default:
cout<<” Given letter is not a vowel”;
}}
```

Output:

Enter any alphabet : n
Given letter is not a vowel

6. The jump Statement

- C++ has four statements that perform an unconditional control transfer. These are return(), goto, break and continue but return() is used only in the function.

7. The goto Statement

- This Statement does not require any condition.
- This Statement passes control anywhere in the program

Syntax:

```
goto label;
------
label:
```

8. The break statement

- The break statement allows the programmer to terminate the loop.
- The break sips from the loop.

9. The continue Statement

- The continue statement work similar to the break statement.
- Instead of forcing the control to end of loop, continue causes the control to pass on to the beginning of the block/ loop.

7. LOOPS IN C++

- A loop is a block of statements for a specified task that performs number of times until the given condition becomes false.

The for loop

- It is an entry controlled loop which checks the condition before entering into the loop.
- If the condition is true it executes the body of the loop until the given condition becomes false.

Syntax and Flowchart

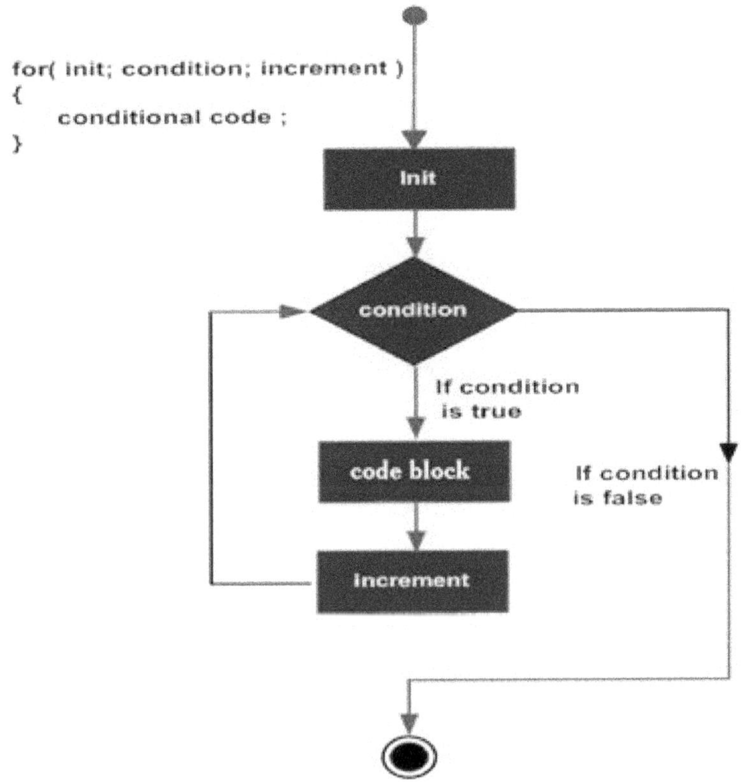

Enter Caption

Ex:

```
void main()
{
for(int a=10;a<20;a=a+1)
{
cout<<a;
}}
```

Output:

10 11 12 13 14 15 16 17 18 19

Nested for loop

- In nested for loop more than one for loop forms a nesting level.
- The outer loop executes first if it is true then enter into the inner loop, the inner loop will be executed repeatedly until the condition becomes false then the condition will be transferred to outer loop. It s the repeated process until the condition becomes false.

Syntax:

```
for(initialization;condition;updation)
{
for(initialization;condition;updation)
{
statements;
}
statements;
}
```

Ex:

```
void main()
{
int i,j;
for(i=1;i<=3;i++)
{
for(j=1;j<=I;j++)
{
cout<<i;
}
cout<<"\n";
}
```

Output:

```
1
2 2
3 3 3
```

The while loop

- This loop is an entry controlled loop.
- A while loop statement repeatedly executes a target statement as long as a given condition is true.

Syntax and Flowchart

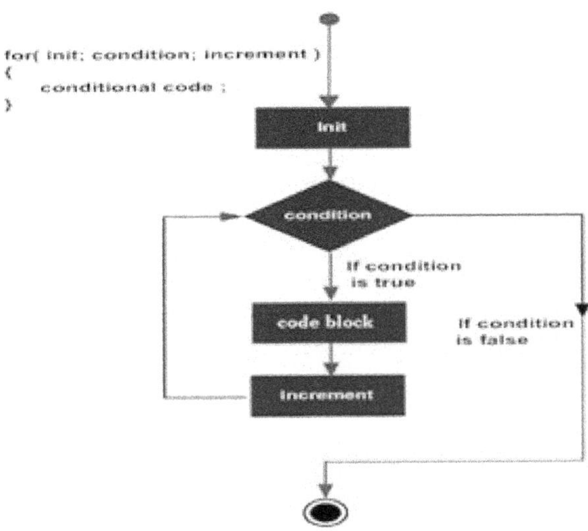

Enter Caption

Ex:

```
#include<iostream.h>
void main()
{
int a=10
while(a<20)
{
cout<<a;
a++;
}
}
```

Output

10 11 12 13 14 15 16 17 18 19

The do..while loop

- A do...while loop is similar to a while loop, except that a do...while loop is guaranteed to execute at least one time because it is an exit controlled loop.

Syntax and Flow chart

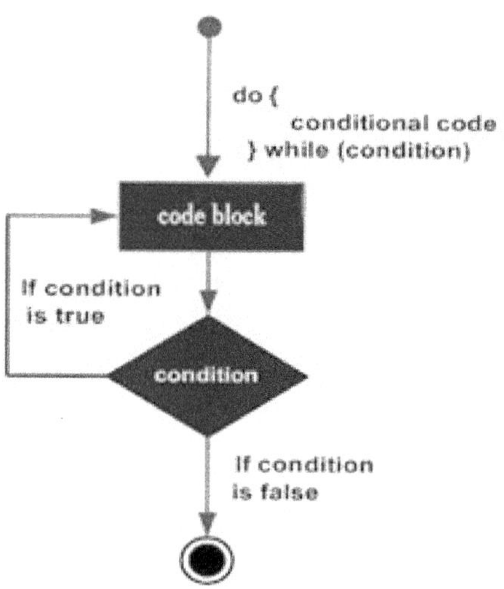

Enter Caption

Ex

```
#include<iostream.h>
void main()
{
int a=10;
do
{
cout<<a;
a=a+1;
}while(a<20);}
```

8.FUNCTIONS IN C++

8.1 Introduction

- Functions are written in order to make C++ program modular. We can break down the complex program into the smaller chunks.
- In C++ group of statements is given a particular name called function name. Function is called from some point of the program
- C++ program must have atleast 1 function and that function should be main.

8.2 Parts of function

- Function prototype declaration
- Definition of a function
- Function call
- Actual arguments and formal arguments
- The return statement

1.Function prototype declaration

- Function prototype consist of function return type, function name and argument list.

Ex : int add(int a,int b);

2.Function definition

- The declaration of a function is followed a function body is called function definition.

Ex:{
c=a+b
}

3.Function call

- A function is a call by itself or any other function in the form of name followed by argument list end with semicolon.
- A function called by itself is recursive function.

Ex:
{
c=a+b;

```
sub();
}
```

4.Actual arguments and formal arguments

- the argument declared in a function declaration is called formal arguments.
- the argument declared in a calling function is known as actual arguments.

Ex:

```
void main()
{
int a,b;
a=10,b=30;
add(a,b); àactual
}
void add(int a, int b) àformal
{
int c=a+b;
cout<<c;
}
```

5. The return statement

The return statement is used to return the value to the caller function.

9. INLINE FUNCTION

- A function is defined and called a set of instruction is created in the memory.
- At each call the control is transferred from main function to sub function. In the passing of control between caller and caller function the execution speed is decreased.
- A function is declared as inline the compiler copies the code of the function in the calling function the passing of control between the calling function and called function is avoided the inline function increase the program execution speed. The inline function in useful when the calling function is small.

Syntax:

```
Inline function name
{
```

Statement 1;
}

Ex:

Int int mul (int a)
{
Return (a8a);
}

Inline function may not work in the following situations.

- The function should not be recursive.
- If the function contain control structure.
- The main function cannot work as inline.

Ex:

Void mul ()'
Void main ();
{
Clrscr();
Mul ();
Getch();
Inline void mul ()
{
Int b=5;
Cout<<"b="<<b*b;
}

Output: b=25

10. FUNCTIONOVERLOADING:

- Defining multiple functions with same name and different data type is called as function over loading or function polymorphism. Polymorphism is one function that has many form.
- Over loading is the function that has different argument list and different data type.

Ex:

Void mul ();
Void main ();

```
{
Int a,b;
Clrscr ();
a = mul ();
Cout<<"a="<<a;
b= mul();
Cout<<"b="<<a;
}
Int mul ()
{
Int a=10;
Return (a*a);
}
Float mul ()
{
Float b=5.0;
Return (b*b);
}
```

Output

a=100
b=25
a=10
b=25.0

Principles of Function Overloading:

Two functions have same data type. The number of argument should be different.

Ex:

Sum (int,int)
Sum (int,int)

- This may be creating duplicate of the data value. So I should be avoided.
- Passing constant value directly to the calling function is also duplicate.

Ex:

Sum (int,int) valid
Sum (10,20) not valid à duplicate

- Passing of arguments function data type should be method while calling the function otherwise the compuiler display prototype mismatch error.

Library advantages

- The library function is:
- Round up the given float value -- ceil , ceill
- Round down the given float value – floor, floorl

Ex:

```
Void main()
{
Int a=3.14;
Int b, c;
B= floorl (a);
C = ceill (a);
Cout<<"B="<<b;
Cout<<"C="<<c;
}
```

Output

b = 3

c = 4

CHAPTER THREE

CLASSES AND OBJECTS

Class in C++

- Classes is a collection of objects
- Classes may have member variables and member functions.
- The member variable and function to be accessed with the help of class objects.
- Class is a same as structure.

Syntax

```
class name of the classs
{
private:
declaration of variable;
declaration of function;
public:
declaration of variable;
declaration of function;
};
```

Ex:

```
class item
{
private:
int a=10;
public:
void show( )
{
```

```
cout<<a;
} };
```

- Class is a keyword it starts and end with curly braces and terminated with a semicolon.
- Private is a keyword the object cannot access directly to the private member variable and functions.
- The public in a keyword the object can access the public member variable and functions and also access the private variable and function through public.

DECLARING OBJECTS

- A class declaration is completed with a help of object.
- A declaration of object is same as declaration of variables.
- Defining object of class data type is called as class instantiation.
- Memory will be allocated only at that time of object creation. .

Syntax:
Class name object-name;
Ex:
Item c;

- A class have any number of object
- Objects is a individual unit it have data and operations for handle the data, object have lifetime within the block in which it is defined.

2.1 Accessing class member
objects can access the variable and function of a class by using dot operator and arrow operator.
Syntax:
object-name .(operator) member function name.
Ex:
a . show( )
2.2 The Public Key Word

- The Public keyword is used to allow object to access the member variables and functions of class directly
- The public keyword is written inside the class and end with colon(:).
- The member variables and function declare after the public keyword can be accessed directly by the object.

Syntax:

```
class name of the class
{
public:
member functions;
};
```

Ex:

```
class one
{
public:
int a;
int b;
};
void main( )
{
one o;
o.a = 10;
o.b = 10.5;
cout <<"a="<<o.a;
cout<<"b="<<o.b;
}
```

Output: a=10 b=10.5

2.3 Private Keyword

- The private keyword is used to prevent from direct access of member variable or function by the object.
- The private member variable or functions can be accessed inside the public section.
- The private keyword is terminated by colon.

Ex:

```
class one
{
private:
int a;
public:
void show( )
```

```
{
a = 10;
cout <<"a="<<a;
}
};
void main( )
{
clrscr( );
one o;
o.show( );
}
```

Output: a=10

3. DEFINING MEMBER FUNCTION

- A class have variables and functions, this function called as member function.
- The member function can be declared with function return type and function name.
- The member function must be declared inside the class.
- They can be defined in Private (or) Public section inside(or) outside of the class.

- If the member function is small it can be defined inside the class and also is called as inline function.
- A function defined outside the class is prototype declaration must be inside the class.

3.1 Member function inside the class

Member function declared inside the class in public (or) private section.

Ex:

```
class one
{
private :
int a,b ;
float c ;
public :
int d;
void subtract( )
{
cout<<"Enter a,b value:";
```

```
cin >>a>>b ;
c= a-b ;
cout <<"a-b ="<<c;
}} ;
void main( )
{
clrscr( );
one o ;
o.subtract( ) ;
o.d = 10 ;
cout <<"d =" <<o.d ;
}
```

Output:

```
Enter a,b value :50,30
a-b = 20.00
d = 10
```

3.2 Member function outside the class

The member function defined outside the class but the following rules to be taken.

1. The prototype of function must be declared inside the class.

2. Function name and class name and its mention type separated by scope access operator is defined outside the class.

Ex:

```
class one
{
private:
int a,b ; float c ;
public:
void Divide (void) ;
} ;
void one :: Divide( )
{
cout <<" Enter A,B value" ;
cin >>a >>b ;
c= a/b ;
cout <<"a/b ="<<c ;
```

```
}
void main( )
{
clrscr ( );
one o ;
o. Divide( );
}
```

Output:

Enter A,B value = 50, 5

a/b =10.00

3.3 Charactertics of Member Function

- Normal function can be invoked freely but the member function called by using an object of the same class.
- The same function can be used in any number of classes.
- Private data (or) function can be accessed by public member function .
- A member function can call other member function without using any object (or) dot operator.

3.4 Outside member function Inlinc

- The Inline function may be inside the member function (or) outside the member function to accessing through objects.
- A member function defined outside the class as inline function the complier copy the statement of that member function and paste into where it is called.
- To reduce the control transfer from called function to calling function and increase the execution speed of the program.

Syntax:

Inline function outside of the class

Inline return type class name :: function name.

3.5 Data Hiding (or) Encapsulation

- Data hiding is also known as encapsulation. It is a process of forming objects.
- An encapsulation object is called as an abstract data type.
- To protect a data using data hiding of the class (or) using private keyword.

Ex

```
class one
{
private:
int a ;
public:
void show( );
};
void one::show( )
{
cout <<" Enter the value a :";
cin >>a;
cout <<"a="<<a;
}
void main ( )
{
one c;
c. show( );
}
```

Output

Enter the value a:5
a=5

3.6 Classes Objects and Memory

- Objects are the variables declared for class data type.
- Objects are a composition of one (or) more variables declared inside the class.
- Each object have own copy of public and private data members.
- An object has access to own copy of data members and to access to data member of other objects.
- Declaration of a class does not allocated memory location of data member.
- When Objects is declared the memory will be reserved for data members not a data member function.

Ex:

```
class one
{
public:
```

```
int a,b;
void show( )
{
cout<<"Enter A,b:";
Cin>>a>>b;
cout <<a<<b;
}
};
void main ( )
{
one e,d;
e.show( );
d.show( );
}
```

3.7 Recursive Member Function

- A function is called by itself is known as Recursive function.
- The Recursion can be used directly (or) Indirectly.
- The direct Recursion the function calls itself until the condition is true/false.
- The indirect Recursion a function call another function called another function.

Ex:

```
class one
{
private:
int x;
public:
x = 10;
void display( )
{
if(x< =15)
{
cout<<"x="<<x;
x+5;
display ( );
```

```
}
};
void main( )
{
one a;
a. display( );
}
```

4. STATIC MEMBER VARIABLE AND FUNCTIONS

- Object have own set of data member variable in memory.
- The member functions are created only once and all objects share the function.
- Each object have own memory location but member function have shared memory location.
- To create common member variable location like function we use static keyword in the declaration of member variable.
- Static is a keyword to store the value of a variable, it is initialized to 0.

Syntax

Static Variable – declaration;

Static member function- prototype;

Ex: Static int c;

Rules of static member variable and function

1. Static data members only within the class not with in the object.
2. Static data members are stored individually not an element of an object.
3. Static data member variable must be initialize otherwise linker error generated.
4. Memory of static data allocated only once all the objects of that class shared that memory location.
5. Static data member initialized outside of the class.

Ex:

```
class one
{
public :
static int d;
void show( )
{++d;
cout<<"d="<<d;
}
```

```
};
int one::d=0
void main( )
{
one a,b,c;
a. show( );
b. show( );
c. show( );
}
```

4.1 Static member functions

- A function is defined as static it can access only static member variable and functions of the same class.
- The non-static members are not available in static functions.

The programmer must follow in points.

- Static member is created in the memory, all objects of the class share the memory.
- Static member functions can access only static data members and functions.
- Static member function can call using class name.

Ex:

```
class num
{
private:
static int d;
public:
static void display( )
{
cout<<"d="<<++d;
}
};
int num::d=0;
void main( )
{
clrscr( );
```

```
num ::display( );
getch( );
}
```

Output: d= 1

4.2 Static private member function

- A static member function can also be declared in private section, the private static function must be called using static public function.

Ex: class num

```
{
private:
static int d;
static void plus( )
{
d = d+2;
}
public:
static void display( )
{
plus ( );
cout<<"d="<<d;
}
};
int num::d=0;
void main( )
{
clrscr( );
num::display( );
getch( );
}
```

Output: d = 2

4.3 Static Object

- An object is collection of one (or) more variable.

- The object is created with static keyword it can be used to initialize all class data member variables to zero (o).

```
class details
{
private:
int a,b;
public:
void display( )
{cout <<"/n Enter the value a&b:";
cin>>a>>b;
cout<<"a="<<a;
cout<<"b="<<b;
}};
void main( )
{
clrscr( );
static details g;
g.display( );
}
```

Output:

Enter the value a&b: 2 4

a=2

b=4

5. ARRAY OF OBJECT

- Array is collection of data items in same data type. The array elements are stored in continuous memory locations.
- We can create an array of object and access the member function of the class.

```
Class one
{
private:
int Reg no;
char name [20];
public:
void get( )
```

```
{
cout <<"Enter the values";
cin>>Reg.No>>name;
}
void display( )
{
get ( );
cout<<"Reg.No ="<<Reg.no;
cout<<" Name="<<name;
}
};
void main ( )
{
one a[2];
for (int i=1;i<=2; i++)
{
a [i].display( );
}
}
```

Output:

a [1]. display
Enter the values = 1000 Ram
Reg.no = 1000 Name = Ram
a [2]. display
Enter the value = 1010 Ravi
Reg.no=1010 Name=Ravi

6. FRIEND FUNCTION

- The private members of the class are accessed only from member function of the class.
- The non member function can't access the private data of the class.
- The non-member function can access private data with the help of friend function.

Ex:

```
class one
{
```

```
private:
int a;
public:
friend void show( );
};
```

- When a function declared as friend function it can be defined at any place in the program.
- The friend function can access any number of class, it can be access private member of an class.

The declaration of the friend function has following properties.

1. There is no scope operator (::) it can be called directly without object.
2. Use the friend function then directly access the private and member of the class.
3. To declare the friend function class name as argument.
4. To define the function outside the class the class name as argument with object.

Ex:

```
class one
{
private:
int b;
public:
friend void show(one);
void read()
{
cout<<"Enter the value of b:";
cin>>b;
}};
class two
{
friend void show(two);
};
void show(one d)
{
cout<<"b="<<d.b;
```

```
}
void main()
{
one d;
d.read();
show(d);
two r;
show(7);
}
```

Output:

```
Enter the value of b:40
b=40
b=7
```

7. OVERLOADING MEMBER FUNCTION

- Overloading is a function have same name with multiple definitions.
- The member function also overloaded like another function.

Ex:

```
class one
{
private:
int a,b;
public:
int add( );
float add( );
void show( )
{
cout<<"a+b="<<add( );
cout<<"a+b="<<add( );
}};
int one::add( )
{
int c;
cout<<"Enter the value of a,b";
```

```
cin>>a>>b;
c=a+b;
return(c);
}
float one::add( )
float c;
{
cout<<"Enter the value of a,b";
cin>>a>>;
float c=a+b;
return(c);
}
void main( )
{
one d;
d.add( );
d.add( );
d.add( );
}
```

Output:

Enter the value of a,b : 10 50

Enter the value of a,b :10.0 50.0

BIT FIELDS AND CLASSES

- Bit fields provider exact amount of bits required for storage of values.
- To using bit field programmer can avoid the unused memory location.
- If a variable value is 1 (or) 0 it need single bit to store.
- If the value is between 0 to 3 it need 2 bits for storing values.
- The array of bit field are not allowed.
- The bitfields have integer datatype, pointer array type also allowed, address of bitfield cannot be obtained using & operator.

Syntax: variable name: no of bits required

Ex:

#define Petrol 1

```
#define Diesel 2
#define Two-wheel 3
#define Four-wheel 4
#define Old 5
#define new 6
class one
{
private:
unsigned type:3;
unsigned type:2;
unsigned type:3;
public:
one{
type=Four-wheel;
fuel=Petrol;
model=new;
}
void show( )
{
cout<<"model="<<model;
cout<<"type="<<type;
cout<<"fuel="<<fuel;
};
void main( )
{
one o;
cout<<"size of object="<<size of (0);
o.show( );
}
```

Output:

```
size of object=1(3+2+3=8bit= 1byte)
model=5
fuel=1
type=4
```

9. CONSTRUCTORS AND DESTRUCTORS

- C++ provider a pair of in-build member functions called constructor and destructor.
- The constructor construct the object and destructor destroy the object.
- The compiler automatically execute this functions.
- Constructor and destructor have arguments like normal function.
- Constructor and destructor decide how the object of a class is created, initialized, copy and destroyed.

9.1 Constructor

- Constructor is created with a name of class, It belongs

Ex:

```
class A
{
A( );
{ }
};
```

- Constructor is executed when the object is declared.
- Constructor have neither return value nor void.
- Constructor can be overloaded by default.
- Constructor without argument is called default constructor.

9.2 Destructor

Destructor has the same name of the class and proceeded by ~(tilde) operator.

Ex

```
class A
{
A( );
{ }
~A( ) { }
};
```

- Destructor can be virtual.
- Destructor does not have any argument.
- Destructor cannot be overloaded.

9.3 Constructor with Arguments

- Creating a constructor with argument is called perameterized constructor.

Ex:

```
class A
{
private:
int a;
public:
A(int x){a = x}
void show( )
{cout<<"a="<<a;}
~ A ( ) {cout<<"destructor called";}
};
void main( )
{
A m(5); ------ implicit call
A n=A(15); ----- explicit call
m. show( );
n. show( );
}
```

Output:

a = 5

a = 15

9.4 Overloading Constructors

- A class can contain more than one constructor is called as constructor overloading.
- Constructor Overloading all the constructor contain different number of arguments, depending upon number of arguments the constructor will be called

Ex:

```
class one
{
private:
```

```
int a,b;
public:
one( )
{
cout<<"a="<<a;
}
one(int x,int y)
{
a=x;
b=y;
}
void show()
{
cout<<"a="<<a;
cout<<"b="<<b;
}};
void main( )
{
one o;
o.show( );
one.m(10);
m.show( );
one n(10,15);
n.show;
}
```

Output:

```
a= b=
a=10 b=
a=10 b=15
```

9.5 Copy Constructors

- The constructor can accept arguments of any data type including user defined data types and an object of its own class.
- Using copy constructor the programmer to declare and initialize one object using reference of another object.

Ex:

```
class num
{
int a,b;
public:
num (num &);----- copy constructor
};
class one
{
int n;
public:
num(int k);
{
n=k;
}
num(num &m)
{n=m.n}
void show( )
{cout<<"n="<<n;}
};
void main( )
{
num x(50);
num y(x);
cout<<" object of x value";
x. show( );
cout<<"object of Y value";
y. show( );}
```

Output:

```
object of x value
n=50
object of y value
n=50
```

9.6 Constructor and Destructor with Static Members

- The member variable is declared as static, then the member variable share the memory location which is created by constructor.
- The destructor to destroy the memory location of the object.

CHAPTER FOUR

OPERATOR OVERLOADING

OPERATOR OVERLOADING

- An operator is a symbol that indicates an operation.
- It is used to perform operation with constant and variables.
- In C++ operators are used to perform the operation with object.
- To perform operation with object to redefine the definition of various operators.
- An existing operator used to perform operation with object of its class as its operents is called operator overloading.

Syntax

```
Return type operator operator symbol (parameters)
{
Statement;
}
```

Ex:

```
number operator + (number D)
{
mumber t;
t.x=x+d.x;
t.y=y+d.y;
return t;
}
```

- C++ support 2 types of overloading
- Unary operator overloading (++,--)

- Binary operator overloading (+,-,*,/)

1.1 Overloading binary operators

- Binary operator requires 2 operands.
- Binary operators are overloaded by using member function and friend function.

1.1.1 Overloading Binary Operators Using Member Function

- To perform overloading with member function requires two objects, the overloading function declared as follows.

Ex: void add + (one A)

1.2 Overloading unary operators

- Unary operators overloading is the operators function to accept the arguments in explicit way to perform the overloading.
- The unary operators ++,-- can be used as prefix (or) suffix with the function.
- This operator have single operand.

Ex:

```
class one
{
private:
int a,b;
public:
one(int m,int n);
{
a=m,b=n;
}
void show( )
{
cout<<"A="<<a;
cout<<"B="<<b;
}
void operator ++( )
```

```
{
++a;
++b;
}};
void main( )
{
clrscr( );
one x(5,10);
cout<<"Before increment";
x.show( );
cout<<"After increment";
++x;
x.show( )
getch( );
}
```

Output:

Before increment
A=5 B=10
After increment
A=6 B=11

2. OVERLOADING FRIEND FUNCTION

- Friend functions are more useful in operator overloading.
- Non-member function can access the class member using friend function.
- In operator overloading the friend function needs the parameters to be explicitly passed.
- The friend function can be called without using object.
- The friend function can be used standard data type as left hand object has right hand operand.

2.1 Overloading binary operator using friend function

- The friend function can be used with member functions for overloading of binary operators.

03=01+02
03=operator+(01,02)
The both state give same result.

y=x+3
y=3+x
both statement given same result but 2nd statement support only the friend function.

Ex:

```
class num
{
private:
int a,b;
public:
void input( )
{
cout<<"Enter the values of A,B:";
cin>>a>>b;
}
void show( )
{
cout<<"A="<<a;
cout<<"B="<<b;
}
friend num operator*(int ,num);
};
num operator*(int a, num t)
{
num t1;
t1.a=a*t.a;
t1.b=b*t.b;
}
void main( )
{
num x,z;
cout<<"object x";
x.input( );
z=3*x;
cout<<"x=";
x.show( );
```

```
cout<<"z=";
z.show( );
}
```

Output:

```
Object x
Enter the values A,B :2 5
x: A=2 B=5
z: A=6 B=15
```

2.2 Overloading unary operator using friend function

- The friend function also support access the private member of a class directly, it can access via object of the same class.

Syntax:

```
Friend return type operator_symbol (var-1,var-2)
{
Statement;
}
```

- The keyword friend define the function as friend for the class, it must be define inside the class (or) outside the class.
- The friend function can define outside of the class but it should be declared inside the class.

Ex:

```
class num
{
private:
int a,b;
public:
void main( )
{
cout<<"Enter values of A,B:";
cin>>a>b;
}
void show( )
```

```
{
cout<<"A="<<a;
cout<<"B="<<b;
}
friend num operator -( num c)
{
c.a=c.a;
c.b=c.b;
}};
void main( )
{
num n1,n2;
n1.input( );
n2=-n1;
n1.show( );
n2.show( );
}
```

Output:

```
Enter values of A , B :10 15
A=10
B=15
A=-10
B=-15
```

3. TYPE CONVERSION

User defined data types and about their conversion to other data type the compiler has no idea. The programmer should write the functions that convert basic data type to user defined data type.

Three types of type conversion

1. Conversion from basic data type to user defined data type
2. User defined data type to basic data type
3. User defined data type to another user defined data type.

3.1 Conversion from basic data type to user defined data type (class type)

- The conversion from basic to class type automatically done by the compiler with the help of type casting function.

- In this type the left hand operand of equal sign = is always class type and right hand operand is basic type.

Ex:

```
class one
{
int x;
public:
one(int z)
{
x=z;
}
void show( )
{
cout<<" x="<<x;
}};
void main( )
{
one z;
z=10
z.show( );
}
```

Output:

x=10

3.2 Conversion of User defined data type to basic data type

- The compiler does not convert any user defined data type to another data type so the programmer externally tells the compiler how to perform conversion from class to basic type.
- These instructions are return in member functions is also called overloading of type caste operators.
- This member function should satisfy the following.

    1. This function should not have any argument.
    2. Do not be a user return type.
    3. It should be a class member function.

Ex:

```
operator int( )
{-------}
class one
{
int x;
public:
operator int( )
{
return(x);
}
one(int z)
{
x=z;
}
void show( )
{
cout<<"x="<<x;
}};
void main( )
{
int k;
one z;
z=50;
k=z
z.show( );
k=z;
cout<<"value of k="<<k;
}
```

Output:

value of k=50

x=50

3.3 Conversion from one class type to another class type

An object of one class is assigned to object of another class is called as conversion from one class type to another class type.

In 2 ways to convert object data type from one class to another.

4. INHERITANCE

- The procedure of creating a new class from one or more existing class is termed as Inheritance.
- A new class will inherit all the properties of existing class.
- A derived class can access all the non-private members of its base class. Thus base-class members that should not be accessible to the member functions of derived classes should be declared private in the base class.
- We can summarize the different access types according to who can access them in the following way:

Access	public	protected	private
Same class	yes	yes	yes
Derived classes	yes	yes	no
Outside classes	yes	no	no

Table-4

4.1 Type of Inheritance

i. Single Inheritance
ii. Multiple Inheritances
iii. Multi level Inheritance
iv. Hierarchical Inheritance
v. Multi-path Inheritance
vi. Hybrid Inheritance

i. Single Inheritance

- Only one base class is used to create a new class is called single Inheritance.
- The new class receives all the functionalities from its base class.

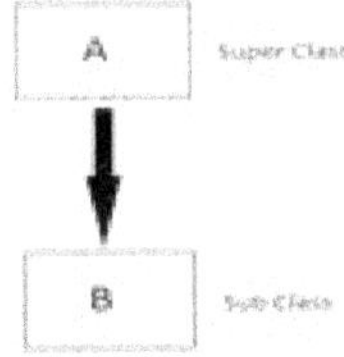

Single Inheritance

Ex:

```
class A
{
protected:
int x;
};
class B: public A
{
private:
int y;
void show( )
{
x = 20;
y = 40;
cout<<"x="<<x;
cout <<"y="<<y;
}
};
void main( )
{
```

```
B b;
b.show( );
}
```

Output: x=20 y=40

ii. Multiple Inheritance

- When two or more base classes used for the derivation of new class is called multiple Inheritance.
- A derived class inheriting the properties of more than one class

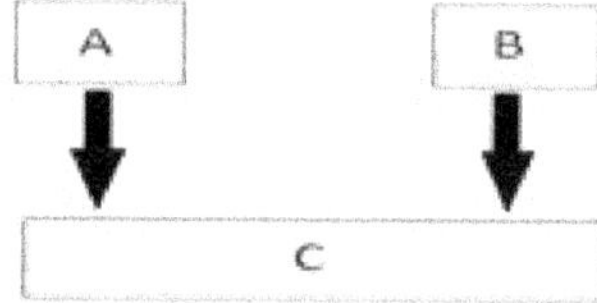

Multiple Inheritance

Ex:

```
class A
{
protected;
float x;
};
class B
{
protected;
float y;
};
class C: Public A,B
{
public:
void show( )
{
x = 10.20; y = 40.50;
```

```
cout<<"multiple inheritance";
cout<<"x ="<<x;
cout<<"y ="<<y;
}};
void main( )
{
C z;
z.show( );
}
```

Output

multiple inheritance
X= 10.20 Y=40.50

iii. **Multi Level Inheritance**

A new class is derived from another derived class is called as multi level inheritance.

Multi Level Inheritance

Ex:

```
class A1
{
protected:
int a;
};
class A2:public A1
{
```

```
protected:
int b;
};
class A3:public A2
{
public:
void show( )
{
a=40;b=70;
cout<<"multilevel inheritance";
cout<<"a="<<a;
cout<<"b="<<b;
}
};
void main( )
{
A3 c;
c.show( );
}
```

Output:

multilevel inheritance
a=40
b=70

iv.Hierarchical Inheritance

- One base class used for create one or more derived class is called Hierarchical Inheritance.
- The several programs require hierarchical arrangement of classes in which derived classes share the properties of base classes

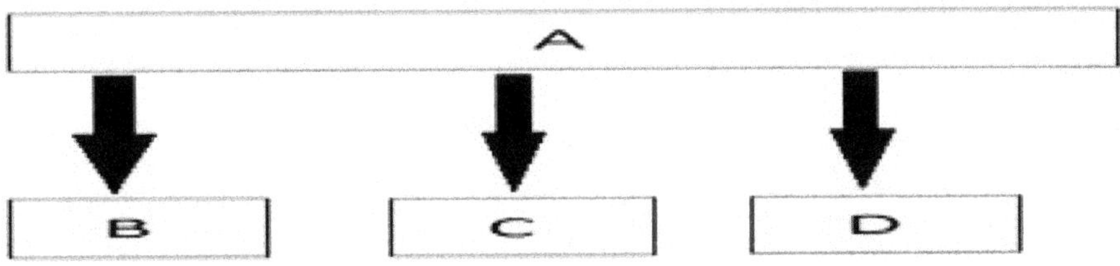

Hierarchical Inheritance

Ex:

```
class A
{
protected:
int a;
}
class B: public A
{
public:
void get( )
{
cout<<" Enter the value of a:";
cin>>a;
}};
class C: public A
{
public:
void show( )
{
cout<<"Hierarchical Inheritance";
cout<<"a ="<<a;
}};
```

```
void main( )
{
B x;
C y;
x.get( );
y.show( );
}
```

Output:

Enter the value for a: 10

a=10

v.Multi-path Inheritance

- Two or more classes are derived from same base class.

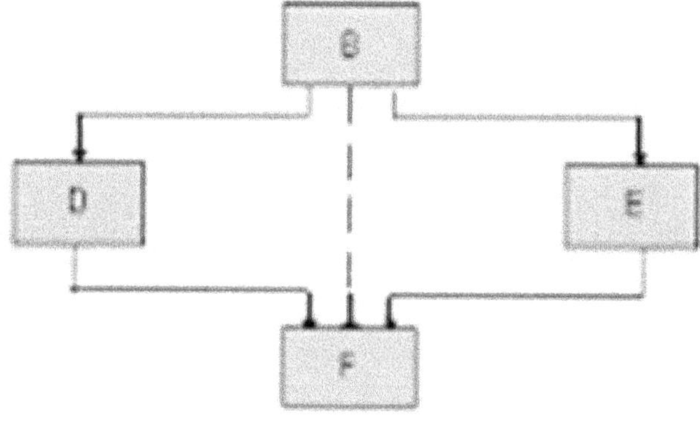

Multi-path Inheritance

```
class A
{
protected:
int a;
};
class B: public A
```

```
{
protected:
int b;
};
class C: public A
{
protected:
int c;
};
class D: public B,C
{
public:
void show( )
{
a=10; b=20; c=30;
cout<<"a="<<a;
cout<<"b="<<b;
cout<<"c="<<c;
}};
void main( )
{
D x;
x.show( );
getch( );
}
```

Output

Error: To access the multiple value of variable a.

vi. Hybrid Inheritance

- Combination of one or more types of inheritance is called as hybrid inheritance.
- A derived class contains essential properties of more type of inheritance.

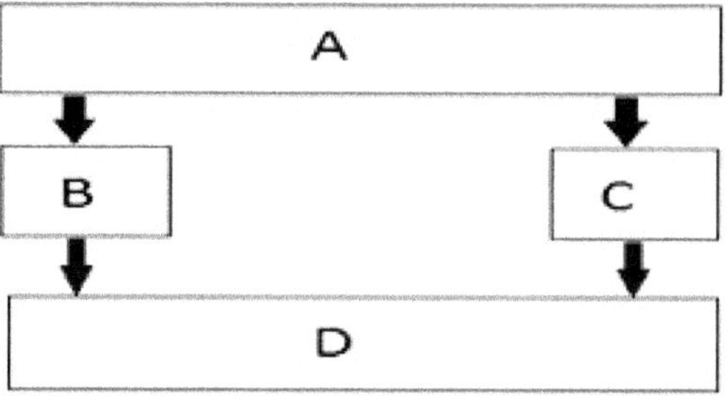

Hybrid Inheritance

Ex:

```
class A
{
protected:
int a;
};
class B: public A
{
public:
int b;
};
class C: public A
{
protected:
int C;
};
class D: public B,C
{
public:
void show( )
{
a=10; b=25; c=35;
```

```
cout<<"Hybrid Inheritance";
cout<<"a="<<a;
cout<<"b="<<b;
cout<<"c="<<c;
}};
void main( )
{
clrscr( );
classD s;
s.show( );
getch ( );
}
```

Output:

Hybrid Inheritance
a=10 b=25 c=35

4.2 Public and Private Inheritance

- A new class derived from old class is called Inheritance.
- The new class access the old class may be private or public class access.

Syntax

```
Class name of derived class : access specifier name of the base class
{
----------
};
Ex;
Class B: public A
{member of class B};
Class C: private B
{member of class C};
Class C:privateB
{member of class C};
```

4.3 Public Inheritance

- A class is derived publicly all the public members of base class can be accessed directly by the derived class.

- The public member of the base class can be accessed using public member function of the derived class.

Ex:

```
class A
{
public:
int x;
};
class B: public A
{
public;
int y;
void show( )
{
x = 10;
y = 20;
cout<<"x="<<x;
cout<<"y="<<y;
}};
void main( )
{
B b;
b.show( );
}
```

5. VIRTUAL BASE CLASSES

- To overcome the ambiguity occurred due to multipath inheritance, C++ provides the keyword virtual.
- The keyword virtual declares the specified classes virtual.
- When classes are declared as virtual the complier takes necessary precaution to avoid duplication of member variable.

Syntax:

Derived class: public virtual base class name

Ex:

Class B: public virtual A

Ex:

```
class A
{
protected:
int a;
};
class B: public virtual A
{
protected:
int b;
};
class C: public virtual A
{
protected:
int c;
};
class D: public B,C
{
public:
void show( )
{
a=10; b=20; c=a*b;
cout<<"a="<<a;
cout<<"b="<<b;
cout<<"c="<<c;
}};
void main( )
{
D x;
x.show( );
getch ( );
}
```

Output: a=10 b=20 c=200

6. ABSTRACT CLASS

- A class is not used for creating an object it is called as abstract class.
- Abstract class is developed only to act as base class and to inherit and no object of these classes are declared.

Ex:

```
class A
{
public:
int a;
};
class B: public A
{
void show( )
{
a=100;
cout<<"a="<<a;
}};
void main( )
{
B x;
x. show( );
}
```

Output: a=100

7. CONSTRUCTOR AND INHERITANCE

- Constructors are used to initialize member variables of the object and destructor is used to destroy the object.
- If the base class has parameterized constructor then the derived class must have a constructor.

Ex:

```
class A
{
public:
int x;
A (int m)
{
cout<<"one argument constructor"
```

```
}};
class B:public A
{
int y;
public:
B (int y)
{
y=j;
cout<<"one argument constructor";
cout<<"y="<<y;
}};
void main( )
{
B b(5);
}
```

Output:

one argument constructor

y=5

8. ADVANTAGES OF INHERITANCE

1. Inheritance provides reusability.
2. The existing classes remain unchanged.
3. In reusability development time of software is reduced.
4. The derived class has the properties of base class so the object allocation is less.
5. The same base class used by number of derived classes, which have same properties of base classes.

9. DISADVANTAGES OF INHERITANCE

1. Using Inheritance frequently in the projects a program may be more complicated.
2. To call the member function in an object is over heads of the complier.
3. The data elements remain unused. The memory allocated to them is not utilized.

CHAPTER FIVE

POINTERS

Pointer

- Pointer is a memory variable that store the memory address of another variable.

DECLARATION OF A POINTER

Syntax:

Datatype *pointer_variable;

Ex:

```
int *a,b;
int *x,*y;
a=&b; // a stores the memory address of the variable b.
```

Ex:

```
void main()
{
int a,*b;
cout<<" enter the value of A";
cin>>a;
cout<<" the value of A="<<a;
cout<<" the address of A="<<&b;
}
```

Output:

Enter the value of A=75

The value of A=75

The address of A=4068.

POINTER TO CLASS

- The pointer variable stores the address of another data variable the pointer variable to be declared in the integer data type to store the address of any data type.
- We can also define pointer to class the starting address of the member variable can be accessed so this pointer is called as class pointer.

Example:

```
Class one
{
Public:
Char name[10];
Int age;
};
Void main()
{
one a={"RAM",20};
one *b;
b=&(one)a;|| b=&a;
Cout<<a. name<<a.age;
Cout<<b.name<<b.age;
}
```

Output:

RAM 20
RAM 20

Pointer to object

- Objects also have an address of a pointer variable can point to specified object.

Ex:

```
class bill
{
int a,b;
Public:
Void getdata(int x,int y)
{
a=x;
```

```
b=y;
}
Void show()
{
Cout<<"A="<<a;
Cout<<"B="<<b;
}};
void main()
{
bill s;
bill *m;
màgetdata(200,500);
màshow();
}
```

Output:

A=200 B=500

THE THIS POINTER

- Every object has a special pointer "this" which points to the object itself.
- The "this" pointer can access all the members of the class except static member of the class.

Ex:

```
Class myclass
{
Private:
int a;
Public:
myclass()
{
a=100;
}
Void print1();
Void print2();
};
void myclass::print1()
```

```
{
cout<<"a="<<a;
}
Void myclass:: print2()
{
Cout<<"my address =<<"this;
Cout<<"A="<< this->a;
}
Void main()
{
Myclass x;
x.print1;
x.print2;
}
```

Output:

a=100

My address=002ff88

A=100

POINTER TO DERIVED CLASSES AND BASE CLASSES

- A pointer which points to the bass class will also point to the derived class also.
- one pointer can point to different classes

Ex:

x is a base class and y is a derived class the pointer pointing to x can also pointt to y

```
Class A
{
Public:
int c;
Void display()
{
cout<<"c="<<c;
}
Class B:public A
{
```

```
Public:
int d;
Void display()
{
Cout<<"c="<<c<<"\n"<<"d="<<d;
}};
Void main()
{
A a;
A *p=&a;
pàc=100;
pàd=200 //not access
cout<<"p points to the base object";
pàdisplay();
B a;
Cout<<"p points to the derived class object";
p=&b;
pàc=150;
pàd=200 // not accessed;
pàdisplay();
}
```

Output:

P points the base objects
C=100
P points to the derived class object
C=150

ARRAY

- Array is a collection of data items in same data type and located in separate memory location.

Array declaration and initialization

Declaration

Syntax: data-type variable-name[size];

Example: int a[5];

Initialization

Syntax: variable-name={value}

Example: a[5]={10,20,30,40,50}

The "a" is an integer type of array and its store 5 integers the compiler reserve 2 bytes of memory for each integer array element .Array element are called with array name followed by element number.

A[0] element number 0

A[1] element number 1

A[2] element number 2

A[3] element number 3

A[4] element number 4

CHARACTERISTICS OF AN ARRAY

- The declaration of int a[5] is creation of five variables of integer type in memory instead of declaring five variable for five values.
- All the elements of an array share the same name they are differ from one another with the help of element numbers a[10],a[1],a[2],a[3],a[4].
- The element number is used to mention each element in an array
- Any particular element of an array can be modified separately without disturbing other elements.

Ex:

```
Void main()
{
Int a[3]={100,200,300}
Cout<<"a[2]="<<a[2];
}
```

Output:

a[2]=300

ARRAY OF CLASSES

Array is a collection of same data type we can also define array of classes.

Ex:

int a[3] -- class a[3];

Ex: Class stud

```
{
Public:
int mark 1;
char name[0];
```

```
Void display()
{
Cout<<"enter the name, mark:";
Cin>>name>>mark;
Cout<<name=\n"<<name;
Cout<<mark=\n"<<mark;
}};
Void main()
{
int i;
stud s[2];
for(i=1;i<=2;i++)
{
s[i].display();
}
getch();
}
```

Output:

Enter the name , mark : Kristaine 100
Name=kristaine
Mark=100
Enter the name , mark: Kavin 100
Name=kavin
Mark=100

MEMORY MODELS

- Memory is one of the critical resources of a computer.
- The memory models have different size of data areas to store the information.

Memory model

1) Tiny 2) Small 3) Medium 4) Compact 5) Large 6) Huge

Tiny

- The tiny model memory have four segment register [CS,DS,ES,SS] with sixteen bit address length.
- Total memory capacity is 64kb. This means that the code, data and stac all fit within 64kb.

Small

- The small memory model have 64kb for code and another 64kb for data.
- All pointers are 16 bit length average size programs use this modelit will increase the execution speed as same as tiny.

Medium

- The medium support 64kb for data segment and 1MB for code with multiple segment all pointers are 16 bits length this model suitable for big programs.

Compact

- This model have 1mb for data and 64kb for code with multiple segment.
- The pointers length is 32 bit length slow access to data and quick code execution.

Large

- Code and data support multiple segment with each have 1MB memory.
- Large model executes very big program only.
- The pointers are in 32 bit length.

Huge
Huge model support multiple segment for both code and data.
The code has 1MB memory and data have 64 kb and stack have 64kb.
Huge model is used in very big programs.
Segment and offset address
Every address has two parts

1. segment
2. offset

We are using address with the help dos. h header file.
Ex:
#include<dos. h>

```
Void main()
{
int a;
Cout<<"address of a="<<&a;
Cout<<"segment address ="<<FP - SEG(&a);
Cout<<"offset address="<<FP - OFF(&a); }
```

Output:

Address of a=0x8f34fff 2
Segment address =8f34
Offset address =fff2

NEW AND DELETE OPERATOR

New operator

- The new operator creates an object and allocates a memory.
- The new operator allocates correct amount of memory from the heap it is called as free store.
- An object created and memory allocated by new operator it is deleted by delete operator.

Delete operator

- The delete operator destroys object, releases allocated memory the delete operate does not destroy pointer object.

Ex:

```
Void main()
{
int i, p;
p=&i;
p=new int [s];
*p=2;
*(p+1)=3;
*(p+2)=4;
Cout<<"value address ";
For (int j=0;j<3;j++)
Cout<<"*(p+j)<<"\t"<< unsigned (p+i);
Delete [ ] p;
}
```

Output:

Value address
2 3350
3 3352
4 32254

DYNAMIC OBJECT

- C++ support dynamic memory allocation using new operator.
- C++ allocates memory and initializes the member variables.
- An object can be creating at runtime that object is called a dynamic object.
- Dynamic object can be created and deleted by the programmer with the help of new and delete operator.

Syntax:

```
ptr=new classname
Delete ptr;
```

Ex:

```
Class data
{
int x, y;
Public:
Void display()
{
x=10, y=20;
Cout<<"x="<<x;
Cout<<"y"=<<y;
}};
Void main()
{
data *d;
d=new data
dàdisplay()
delete d;
}
```

Output:

x=10 y=20

BINDING POLYMORPHISM AND VIRTUAL FUNCTION

Polymorphism

- Polymorphism is a technique in which various forms of a single function can be defined and shared by various objects to perform the operation.
- A polymorphism can be defined at run time and compile time.

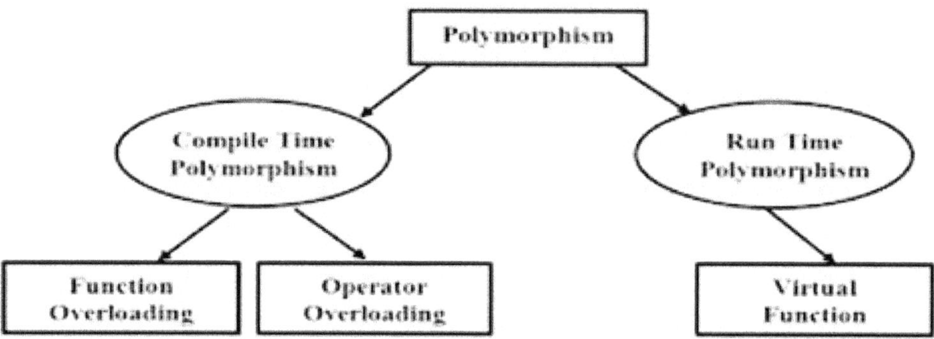

- A function call at compile time is called a static binding (or) early binding.
- A function call at run time is called dynamic (or) late binding.

Binding in c++

C++ supports two types of binding

1. Static binding.
2. Dynamic binding.

Static (early) binding

- The same function name can be used us many places but they should be called with their data type and arguments.

Ex:

Class one

```
{
Public:
int a;
void display ()
{
a=10;
cout<<"a="<<a;
}};
Class two: public one
{
Public:
int b;
Void display()
{
a=10;
b=20;
cout<<"a="<<a;
cout<<"b="<<b;
}};
Void main()
{
Two T;
T.display()
}
```

Output:

a=10

b=20

Dynamic (late) binding

- In Dynamic binding the member functions is defined using the keyword virtual to avoid the duplication.
- The member function followed by the virtual keyword is called as virtual function.

Ex:

```
Class one
{
```

```
Public:
int a;
virtual void display()
{
a=40;
cout<<"a="<<a;
}};
Class two: public one
{
Public:
int b;
virtual void display()
{
a=10;
b=20;
cout<<"a="<<a;
cout<<'b="<<b;
}};
Void main()
{
Two T;
Display();
}
```

Virtual function

- Virtual function of basic class must be redefined in the derived class.
- The programmer can define a virtual function in a base class the same name can be used in derived class even if the number and type arguments are matching.
- Virtual function can only be member function and cannot be access outside the class.

Ex:

```
Class one
{
public:
Virtual void display()
```

```
{
Cout<<"base class";
}};
Class two: public one
{
Public:
Void display()
{
Cout<<"derived class";
}};
Void main()
{
One o;
o. display();
two. T;
T. display();
}
```

Output:

Base class

Derived class

Array of pointers

- Polymorphism refers to dynamic binding that is the selection of function is decided at runtime.
- Dynamic binding is associated with object pointer that is the address of different object can be stored in an array to call the function dynamically.

Ex:

```
Class a
{
Public:
Virtual void show()
{
Cout<<"A";
}};
Class B: public A
```

```
{
Public:
Void show()
{
Cout<<"B";
}};
Class C: public A
{
Public:
void show()
{
cout<<"C";
}};
Void main()
{
A a;
B b;
C c;
A.*p[ ]={&a,&b,&c};
for(int i=1;i<=3;i++;
P[i]->show();
```

Output:

A B C

Pure virtual function

- The member function of the base class is rarely used for doing any operation such functions are called as do-nothing functions, dummy function (or) pure virtual function.
- Pure virtual functions are defined with null boby so the derived class able to override them.

Declaration of pure virtual function

Virtual void display()=0;

- This declaration instruct the compiler that the function is pure virtual function it will not have a definition

Ex:

```
Class one
{
Public:
int a;
one ()
{
a=10;
}
Virtual void display()=0;
};
Class two: public one
{
Public c:
int b;
two()
{
b=20;
}
Void display()
{
Cout<<"a=">>a;
Cout<<"b="<<b;
}
};
Void main()
{
One *n;
nàdisplay(); // cannot call the pure virtual function.
two T;
n=&T;
nàdisplay();
}
```

Output:

A=10 b=20

Abstract class

- Abstract classes used to develop a new class and designed to well defined class hierarchy.
- Abstract classes containing virtual function can be used as program debugging.
- The developer including a header file for this abstract class is “abstract. h”

Ex:

```
#include “abstract. h”
Class A: public debug
{
Public:
int a;
A()
{
a=10;
}
Void show()
{
Cout<<”a=”<<a;
}
};
Class B: public debug
{
Public:
int b;
{
B()
{
b=20;
}};
Void main()
{
A c;
B d;
c. show();
d. show();
}
```

Output: a=10

Rules for virtual function

- The virtual function should not be a static and it must be the member of a class.
- A virtual function may be a friend function of another class.
- Constructors cannot be declared as virtual but destructors declared as virtual.
- The virtual function defined only public section of the class.
- The virtual functions also return a value like other function.
- The prototype of virtual function should be same in the both base class and derived class.
- Arithmetic operation cannot be performed with base class pointer.

Virtual function in derived classes

- Functions are declared virtual in base classes.
- It also possible to redefine the virtual function in the derived class.
- The compiler creates V tables (virtual table) for derived class and store the address of the functions.
- To define the virtual function in a derived class the compiler creates a V table for that function but it does not invoke the function using base class object

Ex:

```
Class A
{
Public:
Virtual void show()
{
Cout <<"A";
}};
Class B: public A;
{
Public:
Void show()
{
Cout<<"B";
}
Void virtual show1()
```

```
{
Cout<<"B";
}};
Void main()
{
A * a, * b;
A c;
B d;
A=&c;
B=&d;
aàshow();
bàshow();
bàshow();
}
```

CHAPTER SIX

FILES

FILES

- A file is a storage area on the disk. The files can be written, read or updated depending on the application.

FILE STREAM CLASSES

Stream is a flow of data. The operation of file is two types, those are

1. Read Operation
2. Write Operation

Stream Classes

istream
ostream
ifstream
iostream
ofstream
fstream

The ios class is the base class all other classes are derived from iso class.

- The istream and ostream classes control input and output functions.
- The functions get ( ) ,getline( ), put( ) and write( ) used for input and output operations.
- The filebuf used to store the input output operations with file.

- The streambuf class to perform the input output operation.
- The functions read ( ) and write ( ) are used to perform read and write operations.
- The fstream base is a base class of ifstream, fstream and ofstream.
- The functions open ( ) and close ( ) used in this fstream and ofstream.
- The ifstream class to support the input functions get ( ),getline ( ),getg ( ),getread( ),seekg (), tellg ( ).
- It performs the input operation with provide open ( ) and default input mode.
- The ofstream support the output functions like seekp ( ),tellp ( ),put ( ) and write ( ).
- It performs the output operation with open ( ) member functions and provide the default output mode.
- The fstream to perform the input operation with the help of istream getline ( ) member function.

Steps for File Operations

Before performing file operation it is necessary to create a file. The operations of a file involve the following steps;

1. File Name

2. Opening a File

3. Reading or Writing the File

4. Detecting Errors

5. Closing File

1. File Name

- File name the name of the file with extension.

Ex: f1.dat, f1.cpp, f1.txt

2. Opening File

- After creating a file we can open a file for operation. The "open ( )" is a member function of the class fstream, it is used to opening a file.

Ex:

```
ofstream out;
out.open ("f1.dat");
out.open ("f2.cpp");
ifstream in
in. open ("f2.cpp")
```

3.Reading or writing the file

- The writing operation of the file may be a new file or existing files. But the read operation of a files only from the existing file.

4. Detecting errors

- Detecting the error is the task of find out the errors that is the file not found the end of the file to be reached some member function used to detect them.

Ex: eof ();

5.Closing the file

- After the file operations, the file to be closed for the next process to opened.

Ex:

```
ifstream in
in.open ("f2.cpp");
in.close();
```

FILE OPENING MODES

Theopening of a file involves several modes depending on the operation to be carried out with the file.er function.

Syntax of the open ( ) Function:

object.open ("File Name" , mode);

Mode Parameter	Operation
ios:: app	Adds data at the end of file.
ios:: ate	After opening character pointer goes to end of file
ios ::binary	Binary file.
ios :: in	opening file for reading.
ios :: no create	open unsuccessful if the file does not exist
ios :: out	Opening file for writing.
ios :: truc	Erase the file content if file present.

Ex:

```
void main ( )
{
int a=20, b=30;
ofstream out ("f1.txt", ios::out);
out<<a<<end 1;
out<<b<<end 1;
}
```

Output

20

30

File Pointers and Manipulators

- There are 2 pointers are associated with files.
- These 2 file pointers provide two integer values.
- The 2 integer values indicate exact position of the file pointers in number of bytes in the file. Two file pointers are;

1. get pointer
2. put pointer

- get pointer is an input pointer and put pointer is known as output pointer.

4. SEQUENCIAL FILE OPERATIONS

- In C++, file stream classes allow to access file sequentially and randomly.
- The data of sequential file must be accessed sequentially that is one character at a time we access the fifth character all previous and read ignored.
- The put ( ) and get ( ) functions used to read or write a single character.
- The read ( ), write ( ) of function used to read or write a binary data.

The put ( ) and get ( ) functions

- The function get ( ) is a member function of the class fstream, used to read a single character from the file.

- The put function also member of fstream class used to write a character to the file.

Ex:

```
#include<fstream.h>
void main ( )
{
char c;
ofstream out;
out .open ("f1.txt", ios::out);
cout<<"\n C++ program;
out .close( );
ifstream in;
in. open ("f1.txt", ios::in);
while(! in.eof ( ))
{
in. get (c);
cout<<c;
exit (1);
}
in. close ( );
}
```

Output:

C++ program

C++ program

5. BINARY AND ASCII FILES

ANSI - American Standard Code for Information Interchange

- Insertion and extraction operators called as stream operator that handles the format of data.
- ACSII code are used by input devices the CPU manipulates data using binary number 0, 1.

Consider the follow statements:

```
cout<<k // display value on screen.
cin>>k // read value for k from keyboard.
```

The operator << converts the integer value k into stream of ASCII characters. The >> operator converts the ASCII character entered by user into binary.

Read ( ) and Write ( ) Functions

- The function get ( ) and put ( ) are used to read and write character the data store in a character format in the file if will occupy more space in memory.
- To overcome the memory space problem using read ( ) and write ( ) function.
- The data represented in read ( ) and write ( ) function in the binary format same in the file and system.

Reading and Writing Class Object

- The function read ( ) and write ( ) used in binary format and can store the large data in small amount of memory.

Ex:

```
Class file1
{
char name[20];
public:
void get( )
{
cout<<"name=";
cin >>name;
}
void show( )
{
cout<<"name is ="<<name;
};
void main( )
{
file f;
fstream out;
out.poen("f1.dat",ios::cout / ios::in);
f.get ( );
out .write(char*)sf, size of (f);
cout<<"enter value";
out .read (char*)sf, size of (f);
f .show ( )
```

```
out .close ( )
}
```

Output:

Enter the name:
Name =Ram
Entered value
Name is = Ram

RANDOM ACCESS OPERATION

- Data file always contain large information and the information always change information should be updated otherwise the data file not useful.
- To update data in the file in a particular record to find out the location where in the file to be stored.

In c++ support two file pointer to find out the record position in the file.

1. seekg (offset , pre-position); This function used to get the file in the specified position.
2. seekp (offset , pre-position); This function is used to write the file in the specified position.

Ex

in seekg(10);->to read from 10th position.
out seekp(10);->to write from 10th position.

Ex:

```
void main( )
{
ofstream out("f1.dat",ios::binary);
char f[20];
strcpy (f, Random access file");
out <<t;
out. close( );
ifstream("f1.txt",ios::binary);
in. seekg(7)
cout<<"\nstring from 7thposition";
while(!in.eof( ))
{
char ch;
in.get (ch);
if (in.eof( ))
```

```
{
cout<<ch;
}
in.close( );
}
```

Output

Random access file

String from 7th position

GENERIC PROGRAMMING WITH TEMPLATE

- A function that works for all C++ data types is called or generic function.
- Template helps the programmer to declare a group of function with generic data type.

Need of Template:

- Template is a technique that allows using a single function or task to work with different data type.
- Using template we can create a single function that can process any type of data.

Syntax

```
Template class <7>
Class name-of-class
{
Class member and function
}
```

- Template class <7> tells the compiler the following class declaration can use the template data type < > is used to declare the variable T.
- The template class used to declare global in outside the class.

Ex:

```
class data
{
Public:
data(char c)
{
```

```
cout<<c;
}
data (int d)
{
cout<<d;
}
};
void main( )
{
data m('x');
data n (10);
}
template class<7>
class data
{
public:
{
data (Tc)
{
cout<<"c="<<c;
}};
void main ( )
{
data <char>m (A)
data <int>n(10)
data <float>0(10.5);
}
```

Output:

C=A

C=10

C=10.5

Function Template

In normal function template accept any data type value as argument. In member function template can accept any number of argument with any data type passed by the object.

Syntax:

```
Template class<7>
Function name ( )
{ statement;
}
Ex
template class<7>
class data
{
tx;
public:
void show(T x)
{
cout<<"x="<<x;
}};
void main( )
{
data c, d, e;
c.show('A');
d.show(65);
e.show(100.5);
}
```

Output:

X=A

X=65

X=100.5

EXCEPTION HANDLING

- An exception is an abnormal termination of a program.
- The exception occurs at runtime the exception also called errors which occurs at runtime.

samples:

1. invalid argument
2. insufficient memory
3. division by zero

In C++ to create a procedure that detect and sent an exceptional condition to execute the suitable action. C++ exception handing provides 3 keywords try throw and catch.

Syntax: TRY

```
try
{
Statement;
}
```

syntax: THROW

```
throw(exception);
```

syntax: CATCH

```
try
{
statement-1;
}
catch (argument)
{
statement-2;
}
```

Exception Handling

- An exception is found via throw statement inside the try block throw an exception for catch block that an error occurred in the try block.
- The catch block to perform the action to execute the abort function to stop the program execution.

Ex:

```
void main()
{
int x, y;
cout<<"\n enter the x, y value:";
cin>>x>>y;
int j;
j=x>y ?0:1;
try
{
If (j= =0)
```

```
{
cout<<"subtraction (x-y)"<<x-y;
else
{
throw(j);
}
catch (int k)
{
cout<<"exception catch j=1"<<I;
}}
```

Output:

Enter the x,y value =10,20
Exception caught j=1
Enter the x, y value=30, 15
Subtraction x-y:15

WORKING WITH STRING

- String is a sequence of characters.
- String contains small letters, capital letters, number and symbols.
- String is an array of character type.

String Library Functions

1. strlen() - to find out the length of the string.
2. strcpy() - copy a string from source to destination.
3. strcmp() - compare the two strings.
4. strrev() - reversing all characters of a string.
5. strupr() - convert lower case character to upper case.
6. strlwr() - convert upper case character to lower case.

DECLARING AND INITIALIZING STRING OBJECT

In C++ string is declared as an object the string object declaration can be done at once using constructor in the string class.

Syntax

String() -> constructor with empty string
String text;
String text ("C++"); -> constructor with one argument

Ex

```
void main()
{
string t;
string t("c++");
string t2("program");
cout<<"t1="<<t1;
cout<<"t2="<<t2;
t=t1;
cout<<"t="<<t;
}
```

Output:

t1 =C++

t2=programming

t=C++

STRING ATTRIBUTES

The followings are string attributes such as size, capacity and maximum , length and empty.

SIZE() : The size function return the size of string object or number of bytes occupied by the string object.

LENGTH() : It returns number of characters present in the string.

CAPACITY() : It return the number of character can be stored in the string object.

MAX-SIZE() : It return the maximum size of the string object.

EMPTY() : The empty function return whether the string is empty or filled.

Ex

```
void main()
{
string s1;
cout<<s1.empty()? True : False;
s1="C++";
cout<<"size of s1="<<s1. size();
cout<<"capacity of s1="s1. capacity();
cout<<"length of s1"<<s1. length();
cout<<"max-size of s1"<< s1.max-size(); }
```

Output

True

Size 3 bytes

Capacity 3
Length 3
Max-size 4294.967263

MISCELLANEOUS STRING FUNCTIONS

1.ASSIGN():

Assign(): This function is used to assign a string to other string object.

Ex

s2. assign(s1);--s1,.s2 are string object 1The contents of string s1 are Assigned to string s2
s2.assign(s1,0,5); -- The characters 0 to 5 in s1 assigned to s2

2.BEGIN() :

Begin():function returns the first character of the string.

Ex:

X=s1.begin()
X is characters pointer s1 is a string object.

Ex:

```
void main ()
{
String s1("C++ programming");
String s2;
S2. assign(s1,0,);
Cout<<"the s2 ="<<s2;
Cout<<"the begin of s1+"<<*x;
}
```

Output:

The s1= C++ programming
The s2= C++
The begin of s1=c

www.ingramcontent.com/pod-product-compliance
Ingram Content Group UK Ltd.
Pitfield, Milton Keynes, MK11 3LW, UK
UKHW061655190726
13853UKWH00008B/2214